The Lutenist's Handbook

A Practical Rough Guide to Playing Renaissance Lute

by

Ben Salfield

Peacock Press

The Lutenist's Handbook
A Practical Rough Guide to Playing Renaissance Lute

© 2016 Ben Salfield

ISBN 978-1-908904-95-9

Published by Northern Bee Books, 2016
Scout Bottom Farm
Mytholmroyd
Hebden Bridge
HX7 5JS (UK)

Design and artwork
D&P Design and Print
Worcestershire

(Cover picture: 'Luitspelende' ['Jester Lutenist'] by Frans Hals (c.1623), Louvre Museum, Paris).

For Charlotte,
who ought to play
"My Lord Chamberlaine His Galliard"
with me.

CONTENTS

Introduction

The renaissance lute is perhaps the most beautiful instrument ever to have existed. While its original heyday was over 400 years ago, the lute and its music have deservedly undergone a major modern revival, thanks to the pioneers of performance in the early part of the second half of last century – including such masters as Julian Bream. They are responsible for inspiring the many thousands of people who have since become interested in studying and playing the instrument.

There can surely be no sweeter sound than that of a well-played renaissance lute. Each one is somehow unique and slightly eccentric – as are many of the people who play them. I suppose we lutenists tend to spend most of our time stuck in the past and then wonder why we don't tend to fit into what is often called 'normality'. Or is that just me?

'The Lutenist's Handbook' offers a pragmatic look at the noble art of luting: it is an overview of technique, with solutions, hints, tips and information that I hope will prove useful. I have examined some things in more detail than others, and instead of just focusing on the way things were (sometimes only allegedly) done, I have tried where possible to give practical options and opinions so that there is opportunity for the budding lutenist to make his or her performance of this beautiful and still relatively rare music as personal and relevant to the modern day as possible.

Of course, there are many unknowns in lute music, and this leaves plenty of scope for judgement calls. For the beginner, this may add to the information overload that can be both confusing, and for some, quite off-putting. The most important thing to remember is that not that everyone plays in the same way or holds the same views about relatively trivial matters, but that the music and the instrument continue to live, breathe and grow. I aim to do nothing more than give people ideas and information and open their minds to some of the possibilities.

Ben Salfield
Cornwall, UK – January 2016.

Choosing a Lute

The best but most expensive way to obtain a lute is to buy a new one from a reputable maker. Buying 'pre-loved' is fraught with potential hazards – not dissimilar to buying a second-hand car! A cheap instrument can be more costly in the long-term, but there are sensible precautions one can take to minimise the risks of buying second-hand.

The size of lute you decide to play in the end partly depends on which repertoire you intend to play, but I would always recommend that beginners dip their toe in with a 6 or 7-course lute. Many lutenists stick with smaller instruments throughout their playing lives, while some move on to larger lutes after a number of years. I moved up in size from a 7-course to a 10-course after playing for about four years.

Cracks and dents are generally bad things to find on a lute and any problem near the neck joint is of particular concern; but a badly made, damaged, or poorly repaired lute may also have other, less visible problems such as loose or displaced bars – one reason for the mysterious buzzing sounds that seem to have no rational explanation.

Make sure the bridge is firmly attached, and that there are no signs it has been re-fitted. If it has been detached, you really need to know how and why it came off and what collateral damage, if any, resulted from that. For example, I had a bridge that came off and splintered part of the soundboard. The repair work was expert – but had it not been, that area would have been dramatically weakened.

A convex or warped soundboard is a disaster. Upon discovering one on a lute for sale, simply find a polite excuse to leave as soon as possible!

Finally, the *action* – that is, the vertical gap between strings and frets, should be comfortable, and each fretted note should sound clear. A dead note or a fret that buzzes is a potential problem. Courses should be evenly spaced and approximately equal in resonance.

If the instrument appears to be well made, sounds nice, feels comfortable and comes at the right price (always haggle, even in the unlikely event that the price is decent!) then it just might be... the one.

Strings & Tuning

Lutes were originally strung with gut. Then, in 1659, Samuel Hartlib, the famous polymath and neighbour of Samuel Pepys wrote: *'Goretsky hath an invention of lute strings covered with silver wyer, or strings which make a most admirable musick.'*[1] Nowadays there are many choices, each with pros and cons. With a little bit of trial and error you will soon know what is right for you.

GUT

Gut strings are the original and most authentic. They have a distinctive, sweet sound, and are now regular in gauge when compared to those of the renaissance. They feel comfortable but are relatively expensive, not long-lasting and hard to keep in tune. For me, they always feel a bit too chunky, and I must confess that I find the sound a little withdrawn in a larger concert hall. They are what they are, though – the original string.

NYLON

Nylon strings with metal wound basses are a relatively new idea, courtesy of instrument maker Albert Augustine, who was unable to source materials in WW2 and decided to use nylon from an army surplus store. These strings are cheap and long lasting, and hold their tuning better than gut when the temperature or humidity levels are inconstant. I just feel uncomfortable with the sound of a lute strung in nylon. It seems a bit cold to me.

OTHER SYNTHETIC MATERIALS

Nowadays, strings are also made from flurocarbon and a variety of other polymers. I have even heard of some players using fishing line! My personal choice of lute strings are nylgut, which I get from an Italian company. They hold their tuning well, have a soft clarity of sound and feel great. Although nylgut strings are relatively pricey initially, their longevity makes them cheap in the long-term. For me, discovering nylgut was a big moment – and I have never looked back.

GAUGING STRINGS

Most lutes should come with a recommendation for string gauges, from the maker. If not, you need to know the string length of the instrument (from the inside of the nut to the bridge) and the intended pitch of the first string. Then you can ask a luthier to recommend gauges for you.

PITCH

In the renaissance, differently-sized lutes were tuned to different pitches. Sometimes, these were played 'in consort' with one another. The composer John Johnson, for instance, was employed by Queen Elizabeth I among '*Her Majesty's Musitians for the three lutes*' in 1577 – that is, three different sizes of lute. Each of these would have been tuned to a different pitch.

The standard nowadays is a 'G' lute, although some very small lutes are tuned a tone than standard, with the *chantarelle* (highest-pitch single string) tuned in A. Of course these are not modern 'G's or 'A's – they would have been somewhat flatter than modern pitch. I normally tune my lutes with the 1st in F#. One could argue that it is a 'G' where A = 415, often considered an 'authentic' early music value.

Thomas Robinson wrote that a lutenist should '*first set up the Treble, so high as you dare venture for breaking.*'[2] In Italy, Franciscus Bossinensis[3] talked about the singer tuning their voice to the lute – because while the vocal parts were written in notation, the lute's pitch might be different. This is by no means the only suggestion that standard concert pitches were dependent on such things as the nearest out-of-tune harpsichord, or the lutenist with whom you were about to play a duet insisting he was in perfect tune and that you should tune into his pitch!

In the early renaissance, basses were often strung with the pairs an octave apart, but by 1610 John Dowland wrote that this was 'irregular to the rules of Musicke.'[4] This is how a 6-course (a *course* being a pair of strings plus the single chantarelle) G lute is normally tuned:

$$G – D – A – F – C – G$$

This may be achieved on a guitar by tuning the 3rd string down a semi tone and playing with a capo on fret 3. For F#, simply take everything done a half tone – and on a guitar place place the capo on fret 2.

7-course lutes normally have the deepest bass in F or D – it may be changed according to the music's requirements. 10-courses is as big as renaissance lutes get. From the 7th down, the standard 10-course G lute tuning is as follows:

$$F – E \text{ or } Eb – D – C$$

CHANGING THE LUTE'S PITCH

The vital thing here is to retain the original tension by using different string gauges. Talk to a string supplier or luthier about this, or check out the many websites on the subject. David van Ooijen[5] suggests a renaissance lute's standard first string tension should range roughly from 33N on a 52cm string length up to 42N on an 85cm string length.

TYING STRINGS

There are innumerable ways to tie lute strings, but I maintain that simplest is best. Before you begin, rub some pencil graphite into the grooves on the nut to smooth the area and prevent any sharp bits that may break one of the strings.

- ▸ Insert the string through its bridge hole from the fretboard side
- ▸ Pull the end over the bridge and under itself
- ▸ Take it over the bridge again and tuck it under itself
- ▸ Make sure it is tucked tight to the rear face of the bridge
- ▸ Slippery trebles (often the chantarelle) may need an extra tuck
- ▸ At the peg end, insert the string through the hole in the peg
- ▸ Wrap the string over its own end while turning the peg
- ▸ Aim to keep the string away from the edge of the peg
- ▸ The string should hold securely in place without a knot

The other method is simply to copy the usual classical guitar style, which also works perfectly well. If you start with the basses, you can tuck the extra bit at the bridge side under the know of the next string up for neatness. Some people are quite fussy about such things.

STICKING AND SLIPPING PEGS

It is easy to obtain various pastes and preparations that violinists and other musicians also use on their pegs. Of course, if the pegs do not fit properly, there is no preparation on the planet that will help...

TUNING IN

Sit on a chair with the lute held firmly between the knees, facing inwards. Before tuning, gently loosen the peg, and push it back in firmly after. Ensure that newly tied strings are not too close to the edge of the peg box, or the peg can pop out and the string unravel. New strings may take a day or so to settle. Just keep playing and tuning.

Frets

There are two sorts of fret available nowadays – gut and nylon. This is one situation where modern technology is no match for the 'old way': I always use gut and I would never recommend nylon to anyone.

THE PROBLEM WITH NYLON

In my opinion, the only good thing about nylon frets is their longevity – they virtually never need replacing. Apart from that, they cut up strings, and their slipperiness sometimes make the individual strings in a course separate from each other when fretted. They are also stiff and do not hug the edges of the fingerboard, often causing little gaps at the edges that can deaden the note. I also found tying them to be as easy as nailing jelly to a wall.

GAUGING GUT FRET

The precise gauging of each fret is down to individual preferences, but I recommend a first fret around 0.90mm in diameter. Some people grade each fret, moving down by 0.05mm per fret while others have fewer different gauges. My own gauges change by 0.10mm per two frets. Here is a table of my own personal fret gauges:

Fret:	1 & 2	3 & 4	5 & 6	7 & 8	9 & 10
Diameter:	0.90mm	0.80mm	0.70mm	0.60mm	0.50mm

Watch for buzzes caused by glued-on body frets (also known as matchstick frets). This sometimes happens if they are on the large side, or if the smallest tied fret is under 0.50mm in diameter. This isn't something to panic about, although it is rather inconvenient. The first choice solution is to increase the smallest fret gauge, and if that doesn't work, simply have the body frets scraped. This is a simple and inexpensive job for a luthier.

Once you have your lute set up to your satisfaction, you won't have to think about the frets for ages. Now all you have to learn is how to tie them – something that is far easier than you might imagine.

HOW TO TIE FRETS

The actual act of tying lute frets seems to be something that bewilders and confuses many people, not helped perhaps by the incredible number of styles and knots that different people employ. I know of at least seven ways, including the double-fretting style employed by several good friends of mine. This is all well and good if one has a particular fascination with knots, but most of us simply want to tie our frets on in a secure, fast, neat and economical manner.

With that in mind, let us examine a method that uses the smallest amount of gut fret, is easy to get the hang of, and will result in the lute having new frets quickly. You will need the following if you wish to tie your frets in the Salfield way:

▸ Fret
▸ Matches or lighter
▸ Beeswax (obtainable from most sewing shops)

I personally recommend re-fretting the whole lute in one go. There is nothing quite like an entire set of new frets, and it is also a great opportunity to give the fretboard a good clean.

▸ Burn the end of the fret so that it swells
▸ Pass this end under the strings from the treble side
▸ Make a thumb knot on the bass side
▸ Pull the knot until it is very tight
▸ Cut off the fret just under 2cm from the knot
▸ Press a small piece of beeswax into the centre of the knot
▸ Burn the stub with a match and melt the beeswax into the knot
▸ Do not set the lute on fire or burn off any varnish

On most lutes, the fretboard tapers slightly. This can be very useful, as it allows one to tie the fret knot lower down than its final position and then slide it up into place, tightening it still further.

Final fret positions may easily be spotted on fingerboards made from very soft wood, because they often develop small notches, and removed frets tend to leave a mark. In the unlikely event that it is impossible to tell, fret position calculators are available online.

Lute Maintenance

THE DANGERS OF HUMIDITY

Wood expands and contracts depending on relative humidity levels, so it is important to keep lutes at an optimum level of humidity. Relative humidity is normally expressed as a percentage; a higher percentage means that the air-water mixture is more humid.

Opinions vary slightly about exactly what 'optimum' means, but I keep my instruments at around 50%-60%. High humidity can cause glue to come unstuck, and cause warping and buzzes. The soundboard may and rise, lifting the bridge. Low humidity makes wood shrink: the soundboard and back will pull against the braces, resulting in more buzzes, and cracks. Keep humidity levels under control, for lute's sake!

Modern, well-insulated houses with central heating are not ideal places for lutes, and in such places lutes are best kept in their cases (a sort of micro-climate) with a humidifier, which may be bought at most instrument shops nowadays.

My best friend Andrea Dieci, the famous Italian classical guitarist, told me how he makes his own humidifier:

- ▸ Make some holes in a resealable plastic bag
- ▸ Cut a piece from a flat washing-up sponge
- ▸ Make it damp
- ▸ Place it inside the bag
- ▸ Seal the bag and place it in the internal compartment of the case

Thomas Mace suffered from the opposite problem – high humidity. He recommended that a good method for keeping a lute away from moisture in the air was to: '*put It into a Bed, that is constantly used, between the Rug and Blanket; but never between the Sheets, because they may be moist with sweat.*'[6]

The modern answer to extremely high humidity is the dehumidifier or an air conditioning system, but a cloth wrapped around the lute will certainly not hurt.

HOW TO CLEAN YOUR LUTE

First of all, prevention is better than a cure: you should always wash your hands with soap before practice (paying special attention to the little finger of the right hand) and dry them on a clean towel. Try to make this a part of your routine, but don't let it become an obsessive-compulsive thing!

Lutes tend to be unvarnished on the soundboards (although some modern ones may be finished with a very light varnish to provide a modicum of dirt resistance), and resting the little finger on in the traditional style eventually will leave a mark. Some lutenists seem not to care about this (indeed there are those who seem almost to take pride in the dirtiness of their lute) but I personally cannot take inspiration from an instrument that is in need of a good clean!

Except for the soundboard, I tend to use a duster to clean my lute, with spray polish and plenty of elbow grease. Cleaning the front side of the lute is easiest during re-fretting and re-stringing. Varnished areas shine up absolutely beautifully in a couple of minutes.

On an unvarnished soundboard, a slightly damp cloth and a tiny amount of detergent is a good starting point. Dry the wood carefully afterwards with a soft, clean towel. For specific areas of dirt such as the oft-seen little finger mark, many lutenists gently rub the wood with soft tissue paper coated in turpentine or white spirit.

I have always had a thing about the dirt mark, and cannot stand the idea of one developing on my soundboard. About every six months I use cotton wool and lavender water on dirt marks – a method that is not recommended by anyone to my knowledge, but one that has served me well and kept my lutes clean for thirty years!

Of course, you should always be careful when you clean your lute, and consult a luthier for recommendations regarding what to use when cleaning it, particularly on the soundboard. Despite the fact that lutes are very light to hold and quite delicate in their construction, a properly built lute won't just fall apart – they were around in rather harder times than the 21st century – and, if it should do so, you need to go and have a serious chat with the person from whom you bought it.

IDENTIFYING AND SOLVING PROBLEMS

At some point, most lutenists experience some kind of problem with their instrument, and lutes are expensive things – so the tendency is to react with a certain amount of alarm, and even full-scale panic. My mantra for such moments is *'there are no problems – only solutions'*, and it is worth remembering that relatively few of them require professional help from your friendly neighbourhood luthier.

It is important to be able to identify and correct problems. In order to become a really good lutenist, you must be vigilant in a whole variety of ways, and this is one of them. Keep your eyes open for anything that doesn't feel, look, sound or seem correct, comfortable or logical. These are the sorts of things that are symptomatic of a problem.

The best way to solve a problem with your lute is to use cold, hard logic. Being dispassionate is not easy, but there are times when it may save you from requiring medical treatment! Here is a brief example of problem-solving on a lute. You should adapt it to fit both physical problems with the instrument, and any problems you have in playing a piece, or mastering a particular technique.

Symptom:
Buzzing note or notes. This is just annoying at first, but can become frustrating and worrying if it continues.

Some possible causes:
- Playing technique – check your left hand fingers
- Badly tied fret – try replacing the fret in question
- Wrong fret gauge – check your gauges
- Fraying fret – try replacing the fret in question
- Body (matchstick) fret is too thick or glue is coming unstuck
- Vibration from a string end – cut off any frayed ends or replace the string
- An old string starting to fall apart – replace the string
- Dust or dirt on the fretboard – clean the fretboard
- Something inside the lute coming literally unstuck – seek help

Remember, the buzzing note is a symptom, not a problem. The problem *causes* the buzzing note, the solution *stops* it.

Holding a Lute

Lutes have the unfair reputation of being tricky to hold. In actual fact, once the student gets used to their chosen method, lutes are more natural to hold than guitars. Consider all the options carefully before making a final decision on how to hold your lute.

In addition to those listed here, there are many methods that should certainly not be attempted, including the historically documented but in my opinion appalling method of resting the lute against the edge of a table. Whichever method you decide on, please just don't do that. Ever!

If the lute seems to slip when you hold it, an anti-slip device may be placed upon the thigh for extra stability. Commonly, a peice of chamois leather or foam are used, but my friend Alyx Ayto suggested a far better alternative: non-stick carpet gripper. I was shocked to see several students in a series of masterclasses I gave in Poland a few weeks later were already using the aforementioned carpet gripper – before I had chance to patent the idea! The anti-slip device may be as invaluable a piece of lute kit to some lutenists as my personal footstool is to me.

When deciding how to sit, you should consider everything with care. The more time and consideration you give to such matters at the start of your lute-playing, the fewer problems you will have later on. The human body simply does not react well when put under stress for long periods of time, and so some important things to remember might include:

- ▶ Chairs with arms make playing the lute awkward
- ▶ Chairs that are the wrong height for you are bad for you
- ▶ Always look downwards at the music on a stand
- ▶ Use a cushion to lessen muscle tension in the gluteal area
- ▶ Keep your back as straight as possible
- ▶ Avoid unnecessary tension to tendons and muscles
- ▶ A good overall body balance results in less muscular work

Let us look at some key methods of holding a lute. These by no means form an exhaustive list, but they are perhaps the most popular for a reason.

"The Lute Player" by Orazio Gentileschi (1563-1639).
The young lady in this painting from around 1612 doesn't quite hold her
lute according to any of the methods described in this book...

THE CROSSED LEG

This was a very common method when I began playing and I remember my teacher using it – and so naturally, I did too. It seems not to be so popular nowadays, but I still know many lutenists who use it.

Primary Method:

This refers to the left leg crossing the right above the knee, creating a neat triangle where the lute may be rested in a balanced manner and without much effort. Your right foot should be flat on the ground. I was able to hold the lute in the triangle without using hands for support, such is the potential stability of this position. Most people who play in this way use an anti-slip aid as mentioned previously.

Secondary Method:

Playing with the right leg crossed over the left and the lute placed upon the right thigh is also possible, and creates a not dissimilar lute position to using a footstool in the 'Spanish' style.

Pros & Cons:

Left leg over right is comfortable and encourages good posture, and the basic position is easy to adapt for various right hand techniques. The biggest problem is paraesthesia ('pins and needles'), and some medics have linked it to pelvic rotation, lumbar and neck pain, and indirectly to varicose veins.

The right leg over left provides momentary relief for anyone who is overcome with paraesthesia, but it is unbalanced and promotes hunching, in addition to the potential medical issues listed above.

Conclusion:

'Left leg over right' starts off as a comfortable way to play... but after five or ten minutes the pins and needles start to creep in. With the amount of time I spend holding a lute, after about five years I abandoned this method – albeit with a certain amount of regret. The secondary method of 'right leg over left' has so few advantages and so many disadvantages that I rate it the lowest of the six methods listed here.

Overall, I would say that the risks and paraesthesia outweigh the benefits with the crossed leg, and so I do not personally recommend it for normal use.

THE STRAP

Many of the lutenists I know nowadays use a strap and swear by it. It seems to be the 'modern' way to hold a lute. I don't recall it being as popular a few years ago – maybe it's a lute fashion thing.

Primary Method:

Usually, the lutenist sits with both feet flat on the ground, without particular physical support for the lute from below, and allows the strap to provide the support and stability. Some people undo the strap at one end and sit on it, feeding a bit out as required, to allow for increased flexibility of position.

Secondary Method:

A less common method of using a strap, is to stand up to play – in what I call 'minstrel style'. When employing this method please double-check that the strap is securely attached at both ends – and whatever you do, don't snag your tights!

Pros & Cons:

Sitting with the strap provides stability and support, and the position encourages good posture. The downside is that it is rather inflexible unless the strap is too loose to provide support, at which point it becomes superfluous. Sitting on the end of an undone strap seems rather one-way – you can always release a bit more strap, but you cannot feed it back in whilst playing. Standing may solve all seated posture problems, but I dislike the 'travelling minstrel' look and the rigidity of the angle of the lute to the body. When I play, the lute becomes an extension of me, so to 'chain' it to me feels quite odd.

Conclusion:

I need more flexibility and freedom of movement than the strap provides, and I dislike both the look and feel of these positions. Sitting on one end of a partly undone strap and feeding a bit out as required seems to me a little extreme for the concert hall. I would not stand to play, but I have never heard of anyone suffering medical problems from doing so.

Overall, there is nothing wrong with this position – but it simply isn't for me. I cannot feel both comfortable and secure relying on the strap.

THE FOOTSTOOL

I don't know anybody who is ambivalent about this position. Perhaps it is the potential for bad posture, or the fact that – as far as I am aware – the footstool is not something that was used in the renaissance. Either way, some people love them and others hate them!

Primary Method:

Place the left foot on a footstool to raise the left thigh to a comfortable height and rest the lute there, with the right foot resting flat on the ground. Slight pressure from the right forearm on the top of the lute gives extra balance. I call this the *classical* style, as it is very similar to the method used by most classical guitarists.

Secondary Method:

Raise the right hand side instead of the left, and rest the lute on the right thigh. I call this the *Spanish* style, as it is very similar to how many flamenco guitarists hold their guitars.

Pros & Cons:

These are both intimate ways to hold a lute that allows ultimate flexibility of movement. They are both very stable, but require awareness of posture as it is easy to hunch over a lute rather than sitting straight. The classical style has been used successfully by guitarists for many years, there are no other potential pitfalls that I am aware of, and it a particularly good method if one is playing a larger instrument. The Spanish style is actually surprisingly stable. With either method, if the gastrocnemius (major calf muscle) is on the tight side, consider pointing the footstool downwards to reduce tension there and in the achilles tendon. I started doing this about a year ago as it is good to keep muscle tension down when engaging in long practice sessions.

Conclusion:

I use the Spanish style myself. I find that the classical style constricts my internal organs, makes me hunch over the lute, and leaves me breathless. In contrast, the Spanish style encourages a straighter back and gives me the ultimate freedom and flexibility of movement.

It may not be for everyone, but I personally prefer it to any other that I have tried over the last thirty years.

Lute Tablature

There are a number of styles of tablature associated with lute playing in the renaissance, although in fact most lutenists tend only to bother with one or two types. There may yet be other systems waiting to be discovered: it is only quite recently, for example, that the mysterious lute music fragment known as the *Wolfenbüttel Manuscript* was found, with a previously unknown tablature dating from about 1460.

Most classical musicians are familiar with notation, which tells the musician which sounds are to be made. Tablature looks at music from a different angle: it tells the musician how to make those sounds. Most tablature is a diagrammatic representation of the courses to be plucked, and the frets to be stopped.

Except for in German tablature, a six-line staff indicates the courses, and signs (or *glyphs*) on the stave represent frets. Rhythm signs are shown above the stave, and are the same as those used in notation but without the ball end. Sometimes, individual notes are marked, or rhythm signs are beamed together (for example, the English Elizabethans had a penchant for lots of flags all joined together); but I prefer a minimalist system where signs are shown at the start of a measure and at rhythm changes. Sometimes, signs are only shown when the rhythm changes.

One issue in renaissance lute music is that of tempo. The renaissance note had a much shorter temporal value than its modern equivalent. I consider that, on average, the ratio is approximately 2:1, but individual composers' habits and the style of piece should also be taken into account, as should your own taste and ability.

Perhaps the biggest problem with lute tablature is the number of variant styles and the fact that scribes and printers had their own idiosyncrasies.

I am not going to argue the pros and cons of using tablature in general, but there are certainly more advantages than disadvantages to tablature when it comes to playing the lute. Tablature is great for this instrument, and is very much tailored to the instinctual nature of the music, and the information included on a tablature sheet is as detailed – or not – as the person who writes it decides. Anyway, it's how lute music is written!

FRENCH TABLATURE

The most popular tablature form was French tablature. Oddly, the earliest manuscript using it is actually Italian, and it was almost universally used in England too! French tablature uses letters to show which frets are to be stopped. An 'a' is an open course, a 'b' is 1st fret, up to the 8th fret ('i'). There is no 'j', but letters then continue from 'k'. The 'c' is often a Greek script 'gamma' and appears to be sidewards – as does the 'd'. For lutes with 8+ courses, extra lines are added below the stave. Here are measures 30-33 of a famous 6-course Ricercar by the early Italian master, Francesco Da Milano:

The opening note of our example is a two-note chord: Courses 2 and 4 played together, both on fret 2. The last note of the example is an open course 1 played with fret 4 on course 5. Notice how the notes are in the space above the string. This is the usual in French tablature, but occasionally the notes are in the middle of the line.

Below are two common methods of showing triplets. The left hand stave uses a small figure '3' – this is the most usual style, and is sometimes also used over the top of a slur sign when the triplets are to be slurred; the right hand method uses closed loop signs instead. Where the triplet rhythm is constant, the first method is simplest; but I think the second method works best when the triplet rhythm changes frequently.

ITALIAN TABLATURE

Italian tablature was commonly used in Italy and wherever there were Italian possessions. Instead of letters, the Italians use numbers, notes tended to be placed on the lines rather than in the spaces, and the highest pitch course is on the bottom. It is, for those used to French tablature, guitar tablature, or even notation, upside-down.

Here is our excerpt written in Italian tablature, for comparison. The rhythm signs here are more typically European in style. Courses below the 6th are rarely fretted in Italian music, and their system does not have a method for describing them unless they are open, when the course number is shown above the stave.

While this form of tablature gives a direct mirror image of the lute's fretboard, some find it tricky to play from and less natural than the French system; but lutenists should be able to read and interpret the Italian style within their first two or three years of playing.

SPANISH & NEAPOLITAN TABLATURES

Spanish tablature is a misnomer – it is almost exclusively used by the Spanish composter Luys Milán (c.1500-c.1561) and is simply inverted Italian tablature – the same as modern guitar tablature. It should really be called 'Milan Tablature'.

Another very unusual form (most famously used in the 1536 Neapolitan edition of 'Libro secondo della Fortuna' by Francesco da Milano) is the Neapolitan style. It is simply 'Spanish +1' – Spanish tablature where there are no zeros – instead, a figure '1' is used to indicate an open course, '2' is fret 1, '3' is fret 2 etc. If you have just learned to play from Italian or Spanish tablature, I suggest you give your brain a break before embarking on sight-reading the Neapolitan style!

GERMAN TABLATURE

Until the end of the 16th century, Germany used a different style of tablature, invented by the renowned, blind organist Conrad Paumann (c.1410-1473). There is an intense logic to its design, but it scares many modern players.

In German tablature, each individual fret has its own symbol and the notes are stacked on top of one another. It was designed for a 5-course lute, and when an extra bass was added, the tablature was botched to include a concurrent horizontal system on the bass course. On the following table, courses are shown vertically and frets horizontally:

Str	F #0	F #1	F #2	F #3	F #4	F #5	F #6	F #7	F #8	F #9
1	5	e	k	p	v	9	e	k	p	v
2	4	d	i	o	t	7	d	i	o	t
3	3	c	h	n	s	z	C	h	n	s
4	2	b	g	m	r	y	b	g	m	r
5	1	a	f	l	q	x	a	f	i	q
6	†	A	B	C	D	E	F	G	H	I

German tablature has its own variants: struck-through glyphs may appear as a horizontal underline. Here is our example in German tablature, featuring Gothic script:

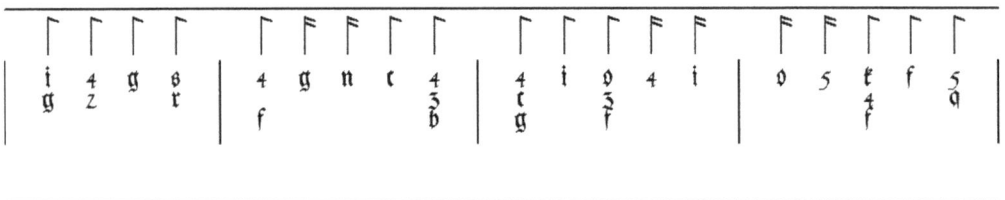

SPEEDING UP THE READING OF TABLATURE

Most lutenists prefer to read French tablature, but whichever your first choice of tablature may be, the way in which you read it will certainly change as you gain experience. The novice player should expect to have to think about and evaluate each note, sign and rhythm mark, but there comes a point when you begin to recognise the patterns and shapes that make up musical sentences. The learning pattern is similar to that of a child learning to turn letters into words and words into sentences on a page. Of course, adults tend to be far less patient about these things...

Recognising patterns and shapes is essential to reading tablature quickly. In particular, it is worth looking at commonly used chords and sequences. Where possible, try to take in an overview of what is ahead over the course of the next few notes and, eventually, of what is ahead in the next measure or so.

BREAKING DOWN RHYTHMS

Many people find it tricky to break down rhythms, especially where there are many horizontal flags on the beat, commonplace in English Elizabethan music. Here is measure 38 from a duet treble, an Allmain by John Johnson[7], which is a typical example:

The first way to approach a complicated measure is to divide it into beats with a pencil stroke, and then look slowly and carefully at each individual beat. In the example above, mark the end of each beat with pencil marks after notes 6, 12, and 20. Take the quickest beat and compare the other notes to it. Count '1' for the first note and '2' for the third note, and tap out the opening beat: 1, 1, 2, 1, 1, 2. Then play the notes slowly to that rhythm before bringing it all up to speed. This method may be adapted and used on entire sections where the rhythm isn't over-complex, as you will see later on in our example piece.

21

CONSISTENT MARKS ON THE MUSIC

By now, you may already be surprised to know that there are a number of marks or signs in lute music that consistently mean the same thing.

Where one exists, the first thing to look at is the time signature. A simple figure may tell you how many beats there are per measure, or the modern standard may be used. Less frequently, the mensural system is used (this is worth extra investigation). Approximately, a circle (*tempus perfectum*) is 3/4 time and a semi circle (*tempus imperfectum*) is 2/4, with dots (*prolatio major*) for compound meter (9/8 or 6/8 time respectively), sometimes with slashes (*diminutum*) for 1:2 proportion. The C3 sign (*proportio tripla*) is a foxy one: it means 1:3 proportion.

Double bars end a section. Repeat dots border the areas between which music should be played a second time although sometimes they are purely decorative in original texts. Where they are only at the end of a section, repeat from the start . Where a measure is played the first time through only, and a subsequent one is played only the second time through, an enclosed figure '1' or '2' (see the section on 'Learning a Piece') is used. A *fermata* may be above a rhythm sign, or stand by itself.

Right hand fingering is usually a single dot for an index finger, with the thumb or middle finger plucking unmarked notes. Sometimes a thumb stroke may be marked with a short vertical line under the note. Left hand fingering, where it is shown, appears as figures, either next to the notes or in a neat block under the stave.

Rhythm signs show how long it is before the next note is played, not the note length, but some composers also indicated note length. Capirola[8] used two small semi circles similar to a curved 'w' to show a held note and a semi circle like a curved 'n' when the player should stop holding it. Other composers used horizontal or diagonal 'hold' lines, or simply left it up to the lutenist to work out.

Classical-style instruction occasionally appear – e.g. 'D.S. al fine' (repeat from the sign up to the end point). Other 'classical' expressions are sometimes used – there are many website glossaries of classical terms for those who are interested. You may also see various ways of showing *bar chords* – see the section on the 'Left Hand'.

The Right Hand

It is sometimes less than clear precisely what 'authenticity' means in lute music, and the waters are often muddied by those who try to be 'authentic' without necessarily appreciating fully the size of the can of worms they are opening. One major problem is that 'lute' describes a whole family of instruments that developed over a period of several hundred years. Right hand technique, for example, that is 'authentic' for a 6-course lute in Italy in 1500 is therefore not authentic for a 10-course lute in England in 1630.

There are those who would validate their ideas about technique, and virtually anything else lute-related, by using iconography alone. While old pictures certainly provide many clues, it is important to remain pragmatic. Artwork is artwork, and not usually intended to be a musical instrument technique guide. We simply do not know whether or not a particular artist played the lute, or how faithfully he or she replicated the precise hand positions of a lutenist. I suggest that we take notice of a variety of sources before accepting something as fact.

Realistically, while it is good to get an overview of the most popular methods, players usually end up developing a 'one size fits all' right hand technique that they can use to play music from most or all the Golden Ages of lute music. While some people suggest that you should not play 6-course music on a 10-course with later technique, it can be done quite successfully except in a few instances – Dalza's strummed Pivas for example. A far bigger problem is getting thumb-inside players to make a decent sound, accurately, on a large lute.

One common factor in the various plucking methods and techniques is the importance of plucking both strings in the course. Inaccurate plucking comes across badly to the listener and makes for an uneven sound, which is even worse when there are octave strings on the bass.

Shortly, we will concentrate on three main styles of right hand techniques used by leading players in the renaissance, and that are all still in use today. First, though, we must consider an important matter that one might normally consider to be more relevant to the classical guitarist than to the lutenist...

NAILS

We tend to think that only the revivalist lutenists of the 1950s and 60s, who often started off as classical guitarists, used nails when playing the lute, and nowadays the practice is rather looked down on. The good news, for those who like the sound of nails on lutes, is that playing with nails seems to have been not uncommon in some parts of the lute world.

Before nails were reported as being in use, but after the quill plectrum had officially died out, there is a report of one of the musicians in a lute duo performance in a letter from Antonio Costadili to Duke Alfonso D'Este, dated March 14th 1524: '...the first (musician) is called Francesco da Milano, who played using two silver thimbles, inside which were two small quills, and he plays so fast that in the judgement of those who hear him he is unique. He is still young, having not yet reached his 28th year.' This is, effectively, the first report of a finger-pick, similar to those used today in Bluegrass music, for instance.

Alessandro Piccinini[15] explicitly said that the thumb nail should be quite short but that the other nails should be longer. The implication here is that at least a bit of nail is OK.

Thomas Mace wrote: 'take notice, that you Strike not your Strings with your Nails, as some do, who maintain it the Best way of Play, but I do not, and for this reason; because the Nail cannot draw so sweet a sound from a Lute, as the nibble end of the Flesh can do.'[6] Things that are criticised or denounced are usually happening somewhere close by.

Finally, Silvius Leopold Weiss wrote to Johann Mattheson (who tried to stab Handel in 1704) saying that he preferred to play without nail, and remarked that the archlute and theorbo sound harsh when nails are used, 'as they normally are in Italy'. Of course, this was a little later on.

You must decide for yourself the route you wish to take with your nails. Nails are certainly to be avoided on gut strings, as they sound terrible and cut up the strings badly; and I personally think there is something rather special about the sound made by plucking with the 'nibble end', particularly when playing with the thumb-inside technique. Do remember though, that people who do things in exactly the same way tend not to stand out. Be different. Be like Francesco da Milano.

THUMB-FINGER ALTERNATION

There are two main thumb and index finger alternation techniques that are commonly used in renaissance lute music, and have been since the start of polyphonic lute playing in Europe. They are the *thumb inside* (or *thumb under*) and the *thumb outside* (or *thumb over*). Both techniques are examined in detail a little later on.

I prefer the Spanish terms when describing these. My style has been heavily influenced by Miguel de Fuenllana (c.1500-1579), the vihuela composer, and I feel that the Spanish were the most progressive of the mid-16th century composers. In addition, part of my family came from Toledo in the early 16th century and so I have always felt a sort of affinity to the musical tradition of the Spanish renaissance.

Dos dedos is the Spanish umbrella term used by the vihuleists for thumb-finger alternation, which comprises the *figueta extranjera* (or *foreign figueta* – often known as 'thumb inside') and *figueta castellana* (or *Castilian figueta* – often known as 'thumb outside'). The name of the latter may give a geographical clue as to its origins.

No one is entirely sure about the origins of the term *figueta* (or 'fig') to describe these techniques, but William Shakespeare certainly refers to the 'Spanish Fig'[16] as an obscene hand gesture, and a lutenist who uses either of the *figueta* techniques will certainly approach this position after plucking a string with their right hand thumb.

Variants of this obscene hand gesture and the sexual swear word around the 'figa' still exist across Europe today, for example in Russia, Italy and Spain, among other places. As to whether it still exists in English in any form, well, I don't give a... fig!

There is perhaps no better way to demonstrate this hand sign than by showing the famous *Study of Three Hands* by Albrecht Dürer, from around 1494. In this wonderful ink study, the artist captures his own left hand in three popular gestures of the day: a heavenly benediction, the aforementioned obscenity and an invitation to courtship.

The rude one, for those who did not manage to guess immediately or who have not yet mastered either of the figueta techniques, is the one on the top right hand side.

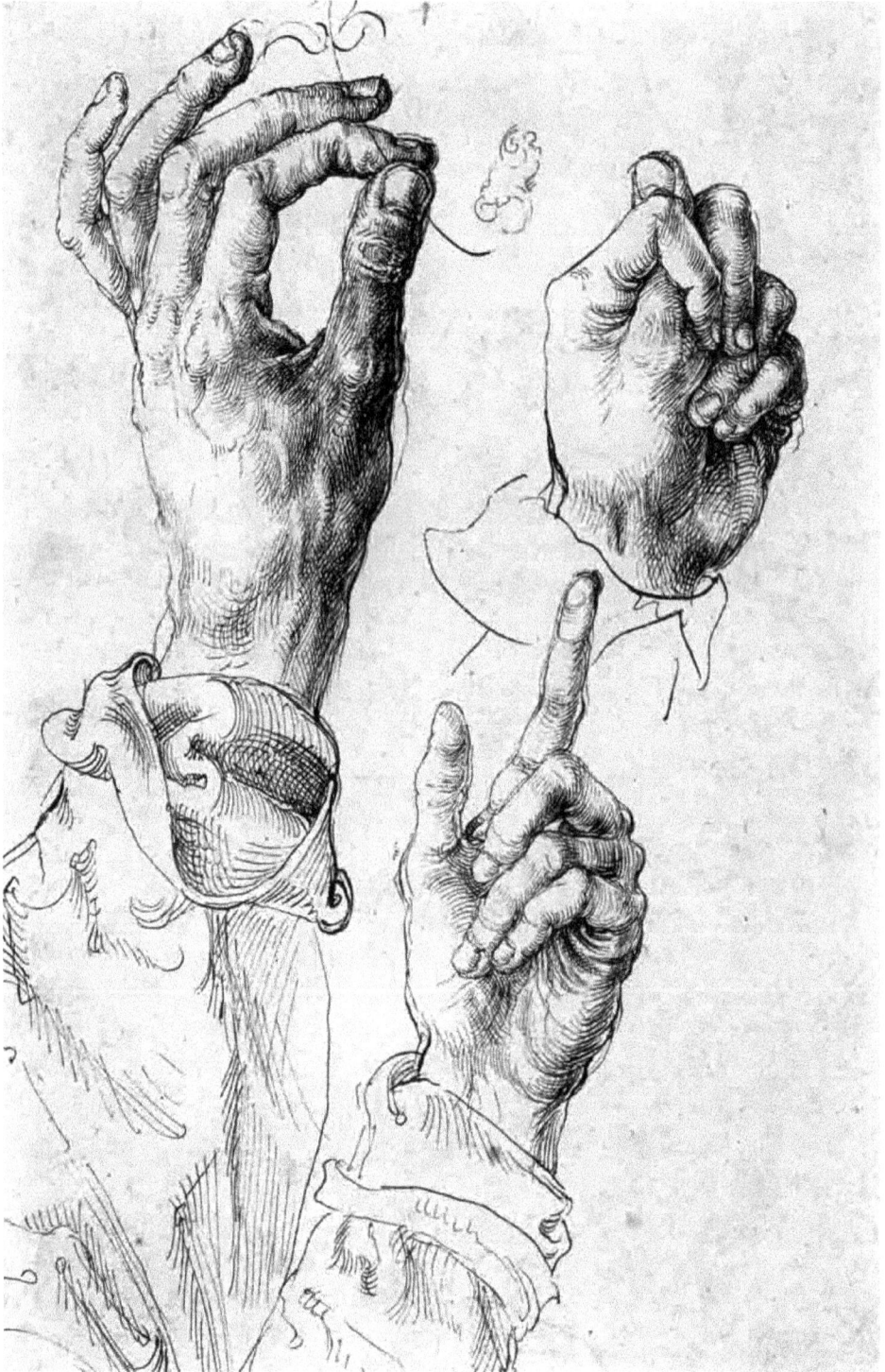

"Study of Three Hands" by Albrecht Dürer (1471-1528)

THUMB INSIDE / FIGUETA EXTRANJERA

The pre-polyphonic lute of the 15th century was plucked with a plectrum – usually a quill. The right arm came round at the bridge end, and the hand followed the arm's line obliquely over the strings. At the start of the 16th century, the plectrum was abandoned in favour of alternating downward strokes from the thumb (for accented notes) and upward strokes from the index finger, but with a hand position that remained unchanged.

When playing using the figueta extranjera technique, the index finger should be slightly curved and the hand relaxed. Successive accented notes should be played with the thumb and the little finger stays on the soundboard at all times. When the arm is at this angle, the natural movement of the thumb should be towards the middle finger.

This was clever, post-medieval technique at its earliest stage of development. The concept of playing chords with fingers set the stage for what was to come. Thumb inside works perfectly well for earlier repertoire on 6-course lutes with octave strings on the basses. For fast passages, it provides a natural position for many people as the thumb and index finger can easily be kept very close to one another, either side of the course. The technique makes a soft, gentle sound, and is very efficient for small, bunched chords, which were rarely arpeggiated at this time.

The problems with this sort of technique only really arises when one is playing larger lutes, where the distance the thumb has to travel is increased dramatically. On a 10-course, for example, thumb inside would not really work.

The figueta extranjera gives the right arm a lot of work to do, but in a natural movement. The concern for me is the wrist. I advise anyone using this technique to be aware of any pain in the flexor tendons, on the palm side of the wrist beneath the transverse carpal ligament.

I personally detest it, but among the many thousands of lutenists playing 6 and 7-course lutes today, the figueta extranjera is, rightly or wrongly, by far the most popular technique in use.

THUMB OUTSIDE / FIGUETA CASTELLANA

By the 1570s, a transitional period had begun where the figueta castellana technique began to supersede the figueta extranjera. This is probably due to musical development more than anything else, as vihuela players in Spain had been using it for fifty years before lutenists adopted it.

By 1610, Besard (translated by John Dowland)[4] recommended figueta castellana for most people. Nine years later, Johann Stobäus (who once described a lute played with figueta extranjera as sounding '*quite rotten and muffled*') included Dowland among a list of the famous lutenists who had changed technique during their careers.[17]

The biggest difference between playing with the figueta extranjera or castellana is in the right arm and hand positions. The arm crosses the soundboard from a far higher position with the figueta castellana, and the hand is held at a near right angle to the strings instead of approximately following their direction. This gives a smaller area of contact with the strings, and changes the entire sound texture.

To place the right hand in the figueta castellana position, simply make a fist with the thumb in the air, place the little finger on the soundboard of the lute and relax the hand.

Figueta castellana is perfect on larger lutes without octave strings on the higher basses (where there are octaves the higher string makes the sound disjointed), and at any point where the repertoire has a more distinct treble and bass split. It allows for more economical movement and increased tonal colour as well as a clearer, more dynamic attack.

The sound difference is the main sticking point: proponents of the figueta extranjera often seem to consider the figueta castellana to be hard, nasal, lacking in gentleness and essentially not lute-like.

Personally, I like to use the figueta castellana for fast phrases on the bass registers, but not constantly. It provides a clarity of sound and a fast, accurate approach, and it is making a bit of a comeback in recent times, as modern players begin to realise that the figueta extranjera is not authentic for all music. So is figueta castellana innovation or ruination? Well... that's for you to decide!

MIDDLE-INDEX / MEDIO-INDICE

By the early 17th century lutes had developed dramatically in size, and the old thumb-finger alternation methods had become impractical. Alternation of *'medio'* and *'indice'* (the Spanish words for the middle and index fingers, terms still used in classical guitar today) began to take over. This was a logical progression in music where the bass was becoming far important, and more separated from the melody, both musically and physically. It simply allowed the thumb to focus on the lower registers without having to move constantly.

It is factually incorrect to describe medio-indice alternation on the lute as 'guitar style' just because many of the lute revivalists were guitarists who adapted their similar technique for the lute. The uncomfortable reality is that, just like the thumb-outside before it, medio-indice is a vihuela technique adopted by the rest of Europe half a century after it was already popular in Spain. If one considers the vihuela to be a cousin of both lute and guitar, it makes sense for players of both instruments to adopt such techniques. It's just that lutenists have never liked change!

The analysis of right hand fingering in Nicolas Vallet's music by Dmitri Goldobin[18] suggests that this technique was in use on at least the first three courses in 1615 for Vallet and many others. Vallet appears to see thumb-outside as a useful alternative when playing runs on lower courses. This also ties in with the musings of the great Spanish composer Miguel de Fuenllana's (c.1500-1579) description of the thumb-outside, as good for achieving a full sound on the lower courses. Nonetheless, his preference for medio-indice was clear: *'in this manner alone resides all perfection.'*[19]

In medio-indice alternation, the middle finger replaces the thumb on the treble courses and plays the heavier beat. The right hand position should be the same as in thumb-outside, but with the thumb resting towards the bass strings.

Medio-indice alternation was an important, pragmatic solution to playing larger lutes, that allows the thumb to stay near the bass register. On smaller lutes, choice is about the style and sound you prefer, taking into account the repertoire you prefer to play. On larger lutes I would argue that medio-indice is the way forward.

ADDITIONAL PLUCKING TECHNIQUES

There are various other plucking techniques, each of which has their own purpose – for convenience or to make a sound effect – but that are not normally shown on lute music. They are valuable additions to technique though, as they provide the lutenist with additional musical possibilities. I am convinced that the great players and experimenters of the renaissance would have embraced such ideas as development, something for which the era was so well known. Shunning musical innovation is a modern malady, not a renaissance one.

HEEL-DAMPING

Heel-damping is particularly common in guitar forms such as Blues, though I have never seen it mentioned in lute music. It provides a deadened sound, by using the side (or 'heel') of the right hand, from the base of the little finger to the wrist, placed down the bridge of the lute whilst playing to stop the strings from ringing. It is awkward to learn, because the position is far removed from that required for comfortable plucking with the thumb and fingers.

PIZZICATO

The lutenist and guitarist Giovanni Paolo Foscarini (c.1600-c.1647) produced five books of music, mainly for guitar in the strummed, *battuto* style. The third of these includes pieces in mixed *battute-pizzicato* style partly notated in Italian lute tablature, which implies that he (as one of the aforementioned experimenters) probably used pizzicato on the lute.

To play pizzicato, hold the fleshy part of the little finger of the right hand against the whole course, near the bridge, whilst plucking. This deadens the sound and provides an effective change in sound texture.

THUMB REST-STROKE

This is a very easy technique to master: after plucking a bass course, simply allow the thumb to come to rest on the one next to it. This helps the right hand find the next course easily when the bass line is ascending, and adds a new dimension to the sound when used discriminatingly. I don't recommend reliance on it, though: a descending bass line played with a thumb rest-stroke puts the right hand constantly out of position and gives the thumb greater distance to travel.

STACCATO

Staccato ('detached' in Italian) is a form of articulation that provides a useful alteration to the sound, but one that was more common in the baroque. Of course, there is no reason to be bound by such constraints!

The *marcato* ('marked' in Italian) *stroke* (an open vertical wedge or upside-down 'v' in notation) and the *marcato dot* (a dot above or below the note in notation) are the types of staccato lutenists might sometimes expect to use. The first is a strong accent combined with a slight shortening of the note; the second has no particular accent. These are open to interpretation. Here is a short example of interpreted staccato, from the treble section of John Johnson's Delyghte Pavin[7]:

Here I would tend to perform the faster notes staccato, against a flowing *ground* (accompanying bass). This sort of articulation highlights a perceived change of mood in a phrase and is a useful performance tool.

The technique I use is simple: pluck the note and then, just before the end of its time, stop it with the next plucking digit. This is particularly straight forward when alternating *m* and *i,* as the hand may be kept completely still and the movement comes from the fingers alone. Bruce MacEvoy's assertion that repeated fingering (a double *i*) *'implies a staccato interpretation'*[20] in renaissance music is probably right, but my fingering is easier! Here is my right hand fingering for the example above. Accents are in capitals and staccato in italics.

$$M - m - i - M - m - i - M - m - i - m - i$$

Those using *p* and *i* alternation might prefer the repeated indice, thus:

$$P - i - i - P - i - i - P - i - i - p - i$$

CHORD PLUCKING

While Germans Hans Gerle and Hans Neusidler suggested in the 1530s and 1540s that chords should be strummed downwards with the thumb alone, they appeared to have been aiming their ideas at beginners, and this does not seem to have been the general rule across Europe. Nonetheless, there are examples, for instance by Joan Ambrosio Dalza, twenty-five years earlier, where the thumb-strum is the only option.

Chords with three or more notes require a little more right hand balance than those with only two notes. Place each digit on its respective course so that both strings will sound when plucked, press down gently and play the courses simultaneously so that each note can be heard clearly but together. If one or more of the notes does not sound, but the plucking action is correct, check the left hand for a problem with the fretting fingers.

The movement of digits should be concise to allow preparation for whatever is coming next. This is something that should be included on your checklist even after many years, and used in your self-critique. Any technique that is not regularly checked can begin to deteriorate without awareness. It is very easy to become complacent about technique.

The following overview describes right hand fingering for chords using the conventional Spanish, in italics: we have already used *i* and *m* for medio and indice; in addition, *p* (pulgar) means the thumb and *a* (anular) is the ring finger. The little finger is rarely used, but where it is we will describe it as *4*.

Two-note chords:

Pluck two-note chords with *p* and *m* on heavier beats or *p* and *i* on lighter beats. Where the bass line is separate, keep *p* near the bass and use *m* and *i* together for two-note chords where practical.

Three-note chords:

Three-note chords normally use either *p*, *i* and *m*, or *i*, *m* and *a*. The former is used except where there is a separate bass line. If the *i* is in use on course 3 or 4 and *p* is playing a bass, in the case of a split chord (where not all plucked courses are next to each other) I often use *a* on course 1. Try out the combinations – it sounds complex but is actually quite straight forward and very logical.

Here is an example of the *i*, *m* and *p* and *i*, *m* and *a* in action when plucking three-note block chords. In the first measure below, the lowest note of each chord is plucked with *p*, while in the second measure *p* is free for the lone bass and the 'c' on course 4, and the three-note chords are plucked with *i*, *m* and *a*:

Four-note chords:
Four-note block chords should be played with *p*, *i*, *m* and *a* from the lowest course used.

Five-note chords:
There is no evidence that five-note chords were ever played except as arpeggios, but there is no real reason why they should not be. You could use the technique described for four-note chords – but add *4*. Popularly, five-note chords were plucked using a double *p* on the lower courses, with *i*, *m* and *a* plucking the higher ones.

Six-note chords:
There are four methods I use to pluck six-note chords:

(1) Use *p* to play every course evenly in a strum
(2) Use *p* to strum five courses and *i* to pluck the first
(3) Use *p* for courses 6 and 5, *i* for 4 and 3, *m* for 2 and *a* for 1
(4) Use *p* for courses 6 and 5, *i* for 4, *m* for 3, *a* for 2 and *4* for 1

(1) allows the chord to be played quickly; (2) provides a clean sound and an even finish to the chord and is my method of choice; (3) is the trickiest, but the sound is different again because of the up-pluck with *i*; and (4) is one of my variants that uses all the right hand digits. You will find that each of these has its own time and place, but that you may well have your own favourite method after a while.

Arpeggiated chords:

While the *arpeggio* (also known as the 'rolled' or 'spread' chord) does not appear to have been used in the earliest lute music as an interpreted ornament to chords, it certainly existed in the early 16th century as a musical feature – for example in some of the works of the Milanese composer Joan Ambrosio Dalza, published in 1508[21].

I would heartily recommend that everyone learns how to ornament chords in this way. The arpeggio can add an extra and very beautiful dimension to many lute pieces; but please be aware that its overuse muddies the music and produce eye-rolling rather than sighs of delight. I really cannot emphasise this enough.

To arpeggiate a chord, use the same fingerings for standard chord plucking, but instead of playing all the notes simultaneously, play them separately but quickly and smoothly. The last note of the arpeggio should be longer than the rest, with the preceding notes of approximately equal length to one another. I often suggest that students begin learning how an arpeggio 'feels' on the right hand by starting with their fingers touching the appropriate strings.

Below, there are example chords in the first and third measures, with arpeggiated versions in the second and fourth. The fingering for both left and right hands is the same on each and the length of the chord is the same as that of the overall arpeggio, but the last note sounds for longer than the rest.

In any form of note ornamentation, positioning and frequency is the key to getting the best effect. The same applies to arpeggios – interpretation is entirely personal but I would suggest the lutenist bears in mind that the most beautiful gems are best displayed with a plain background.

The Left Hand

While there have been many articles and treatises written about the important subject of right hand technique in renaissance lute playing, very little has been written about what I consider to be the equally important subject of the left hand. The right hand took over most of the interest, it seems to me, because of the many technique options available. Without a good left hand technique, though, it is not possible to play the lute well, fluently and with ease.

BASIC LEFT HAND POSITION

To achieve the basic left hand position, first allow your arm to hang by your side, with all the muscles relaxed. Then, bend your elbow and lift the hand so that your first and second fingers are pressing down just below the first two frets on the chantarelle. The thumb should rest on the lower part of the back of the neck, approximately half way between the two fingers and directly opposite them.

The fingers should be gently curved, and not touching against any other string besides the one they are purposefully pressing down. The web space between the thumb and first finger goes underneath the neck of the lute, but should not touch it. Try and keep the arm and hand relaxed and allow the wrist to bend slightly.

Now add the third and fourth fingers of the left hand onto the third and fourth frets of the chantarelle. Note which part of each finger end presses down on the frets. I suggest that beginners should try fretting all the strings in this way, on various frets, noting slight changes in the angle of the hand, fingers and arm that work best.

The ball of the thumb is the best part to press gently against the back of the neck. It allows the thumb to be almost straight and provides optimum support with minimum effort.

One of the most important things to try and achieve where possible is muscle relaxation. This allows the arm, hand and fingers to move in as smooth and efficient a manner as possible. Everything will take a while to get used to. Do not expect it all just to fall into place immediately.

THE PROXIMITY OF FINGERS TO COURSES

Fingers should be kept close to the courses even when they are not being used. The further away your fingers are from each course, the more potential there is for inaccuracy when fretting. This is also the case when playing slurs: people often think that hitting a finger hard onto the fret makes a good hammer, when the truth is that accuracy is far more important – as you will see later on.

THE IMPORTANCE OF THE THUMB

I think the thumb is possibly the most under-rated digit of the left hand. In most walks of life, someone at the front takes the credit while it is the person behind the scenes who made things happen. The same is true of the left hand. Without thumbs, we would be in big trouble.

The left hand thumb has a single, vital role: to provide proper support and guidance to the fingers and left hand. The thumb should be relaxed and its movements fluid. It should join the the rest of the hand in moving up and down the fretboard, and neither be left behind nor overtake the fingers.

The primary finger in a hand position is the one that creates the stability, and is normally the one that stays in position while others are moving. This finger – usually the first or second – will naturally be pressed down a little harder than the others and is normally given the most support by the thumb, which should stay roughly behind it.

Always be careful that you don't grip onto the back of the neck with the thumb – it does nothing useful and adds unwanted tension into the hand. Try to use the thumb as a counter-balance and allow it to lift off momentarily during some positional changes so that any tension may naturally be dispersed.

The thumb's movement should be both horizontal and vertical. When the hand has to stretch a long way – for example if fingers are on both the third and seventh frets, the thumb should be moved slightly to the right to give a little extra reach. In bar chords (see the next page) you will find that the thumb often moves vertically downwards. The most important thing of all is that the thumb is flexible and able to move about in a relaxed manner where necessary. Keep an eye on what your thumb gets up to, and train it to be in the right place at the right time.

BAR CHORDS

A *bar chord* (also known as a 'barre') is a chord where the first finger presses down the frets on more than one course simultaneously. It does this by pressing the finger across the courses and fretting the deepest note with the tip of the finger.

I tend to describe a bar chord by the number of courses to be covered rather than using the commonly used guitar terms, such as *partial* or *half* bar for those bar chords that do not cover the whole six strings on a guitar. It makes more sense in any case to describe accurately the number of strings to be covered: there is no doubt when the chord is described as a 'four course bar'.

The technique for playing bar chords is not difficult to master; unfortunately, though, it is one of the worst taught and most troublesome techniques for a student who simply doesn't know how to approach it. Trying to correct bad bar technique is not the easiest, so it is far better to learn it properly to begin with.

One of the most important parts of bar technique concerns the thumb, which should be approximately half a fret to the right of the bar finger, with the thumb tip pressing from low on the back of the neck in the direction of the tip of the first finger. The thumb, as the strongest digit, should take approximately two-thirds of the pressure, and the finger one-third. It is possible to make a vice-like grip this way, but it is not necessary to press down as hard as people often imagine.

The importance of the thumb cannot be over-emphasised when playing the chords. A well positioned thumb provides not only the strength but also the leverage that ensures a good, clear bar. My friend Jeffrey Goodman, who taught classical guitar at the University of California for many years, says that 'more often than not, poor results... come from lack of leverage rather than lack of strength.'[21]

Never push the bar finger down with another finger – that is simply a sign that the bar technique is flawed and leads to a variety of problems, such as impacting negatively on the flexibility of the left hand. It is also important not to press too hard with the bar finger, because that too can impact negatively on the sound.

A bar chord may be shown in a variety of ways in lute music:

- ▶ A letter 'C' for 'capo' and a fret number (often Roman numerals)
- ▶ A letter 'B' for 'bar' (especially common in the USA)
- ▶ A square bracket on the left hand side of the chord
- ▶ Fingering that shows the first finger apparently being used twice

Note that Roman numerals shown above the music without a letter 'C' usually (but not always!) indicates a hand position – in other words, by which fret the first finger should be – rather than a bar. This is most commonly seen in guitar music, but this also occurs in some modern lute editions.

Quite often there is no indication on the music that a bar chord should be played, and you just have to recognise the situation when it is to be used. This becomes apparent with experience, but typical situations to watch out for are where five or more strings are supposed to be fretted in a single chord – which was how I first stumbled upon the existence of the bar chord, aged 13…

If the bar chord does not sound right, you should check the following to find out what is going wrong:

- ▶ Is the thumb positioned correctly?
- ▶ Are you squeezing the thumb and finger together hard enough?
- ▶ Are you squeezing the thumb and finger together too hard?
- ▶ Is the finger close enough to the fret?
- ▶ Is the finger going over the fret?
- ▶ Does a crease or gap on a finger joint coincide with a string?

The good thing is, any problems are easy to correct. The most common ones are caused by finger creases and joint gaps. These are bits of the finger that just don't push down strings. Simply move the vertical position of the finger very slightly until finger – rather than 'gap' – covers each string, and every course is being pushed down cleanly.

Something you should NOT do is practice bar chords for long periods. It can become painful in a relatively short space of time, and I advise students not to do anything to the point of real pain. Bar chords are not the easiest at first, but they will come in time if your technique is good.

MOVING UP AND DOWN THE FRETBOARD

It is important to keep your movements concise as you move the left hand up and down the fretboard. For example, when moving from fretting the 'd' on the first string with a first finger to fretting the 'h' on the same string with the little finger, the hand's move should be made in a smooth, slightly arced line, without random fingers moving about.

Always pull the hand up and down the frets, never push it. In the above example, the movement action should come from the little finger. In the reverse move, going from the 'h' to the 'd', the movement action should come from the first finger. Pushed hands have a curious tendency to overshoot frets, while pulled hands are more accurate.

BALANCE

Of course, balance is something that affects all the things I have talked about with the left hand so far; but it is also something that should be considered by itself. A balanced, straight hand, that is comfortable in its positions and controlled in its movements, is a hand that will serve you well in your music-making.

THE ORDER OF FINGERS

This is part of the mechanics of left hand movement. Moving from one position on the fretboard to another isn't simply a matter of assuming a position, taking the fingers off and then assuming another. It is far more subtle than that. For example, where a finger will be used on more than one note, it can often stay in position while the others move around it. It is more economical to build positions where possible rather than changing an entire hand position.

Choosing the order of the movement of fingers is of vital importance. There are no 'rules' for this as such, but the 'leading' finger – the fretting finger furthest towards the direction of movement – or a fretting finger involved in the next note to be plucked, are likely candidates. Often, in a bar chord, it is actually better to place the bar after the other fingers have been arranged in position. If the bar finger is placed first, the fingers can struggle to find their frets.

Of course, do remember that the fingers are only placed on frets literally a fraction of a second apart – it is in your quarter speed practice that you should work hardest at ordering the fingers correctly – slow motion allows you to see more accurately the best order of movement.

INTRODUCING FINGER-MAPPING

To end this section on the left hand, I would like to give you a glimpse at the art of finger-mapping, a concept I invented around thirty years ago that both helped me find my way around the fretboard quickly when playing from tablature, and that, many years later, I used to great effect when teaching people with, for example, severe visual impairments.

Just as the concept of tablature is different from that of notation, so our method of interpreting the movement between individual notes and chords also has to change when we use tablature. Instead of thinking about a note's pitch ('play the C on the 6th) we have to think about which fret we should move to ('play fret 5 on the 6th) and how we are going to get there. There is little point in cluttering the brain by considering the pitch of the note when our music-playing instruction (that is to say, the lute tablature) doesn't mention it.

There is no reason why you cannot route your entire hand, working out how it should move from where it is to where it needs to go. If I am to travel to Timbuktu, I don't need to know where Timbuktu is, as long as I know the route I need to take to get there from my current location. In the case of the left hand on lute frets, it is no more than a process that allows for high-speed mental recognition of the necessary movement directions of each digit.

Finger-mapping also looks for patterns for the fingers to remember. Identifying and remembering specific movements and noting when they recur is also good for understanding and memorising music.

As an aside, this is also useful for training the thumb of the right hand on larger lutes. Instead of considering the pitch or the number of the course, look at the bass separately and think in terms of where the thumb has to move to: the number of courses up or down, and any recurring pattern. This is particularly helpful on baroque lutes, where the music often requires playing lots of open basses.

In finger-mapping, consistency of thought process is vital. Your mental or vocal description of positions must be formatted (don't mix up 'string 2, fret d' with 'string 2 fret 3' or 'the third fret of the second string'); it is about conditioning the brain to compute movements more efficiently, and while it may not work for everyone, it has helped many students.

Ornamentation

I always think of ornaments in renaissance lute music as being in two different main groups: those of the left hand and those of the right.

Left hand ornaments where unplucked notes are added to the music are called *grace notes*, and comprise various forms and extensions of *shakes* and *falls* which in turn are combinations of *slurs*. Ascending slurs are called *hammers* and descending ones are *pull-offs* (also known as *snaps*). Right hand ornaments comprise *arpeggios*, *divisions*, and most *effects* (changes to the sound of the plucked note), which are examined in the section on 'The Right Hand'. One effect, *vibrato*, is performed by the left hand, and that is looked at in this section.

Ornaments and the signs used to show them can be haphazard and inconsistent, although the context will often provide a key. There is the potential for plenty of confusion if one takes into consideration improvisation, and the fact that printed sources often omitted ornaments while some hand-written sources seem to have been heavily, sometimes overly, ornamented by their amateur compilers.

The lack of ornamentation in many printed sources does not mean ornamentation was not expected: printers often simply did not have had the appropriate signs in their shops[7]. In any case, players who were laying out enough money to buy music books were probably at a standard where they already knew where various ornaments would be expected. After all, a music book could cost the equivalent of a lute in Elizabethan England.

The way a lutenist ornaments music is very personal, and integral to their style of playing, so I recommend careful consideration and an in-depth look into the many online articles on this subject. As with everything in lute music, the wisdom of each learned opinion is only one newly discovered manuscript away from being completely debunked, so I recommend that taste, musicality, common sense and context should override the words of the wise when deciding on which ornaments to use, and when.

Next, we will look at how to play some left hand ornaments; after, we will examine those of the right hand.

HAMMERS & PULL-OFFS

Before learning how to play graces, it is important to get a bit of the technique under your belt – how to play a *hammer* and *pull-off*. These slurs are rare in renaissance music except when they are played as parts of ornaments, while in baroque lute music they are very common, both as an effect and (in Weiss, for instance) for convenience. The curved line is a slur sign, which can either go under or over the notes according to personal taste. Some baroque composers (Lauffensteiner, for example) used the wide over-slur for a pull-off and the under-slur for a hammer – but they are generally a matter of personal taste.

To play a hammer, pluck the first note and then fret the next without plucking the course. The finger that frets the second note should begin quite close to the fret for accuracy. Try the examples below:

A pull-off is the exact opposite. Here are the above examples in reverse: pluck the first note, then take the finger off and sound the next note without plucking. Where the second note is fretted, both fingers must be in place before the move. Lifting the finger at 90° to the course will result in no sound, and a 180° angle will make a hard sound. Your 'sweet spot' is somewhere between the two. Mace[8] describes the *soft shake* and *hard shake* as pull-offs played nearer the 90° or 180° respectively.

SHAKES & FALLS

The *shake* and *fall* are normally shown in English sources using a hash sign (or double cross) [#] and a cross [+] respectively. In Italy, Capirola[8] appeared to describe (in Venetian dialect) a red number written in dots as a form of shake – and other signs appear in different manuscripts.

All trills are forms of shakes and falls. When playing graces, simply pluck the first note and then combine hammers and pull-offs.

Graces normally move in the opposite direction to the music: ascending scales often begin on the lower auxiliary, and vice versa, to avoid note anticipation. This is described by the Spanish music theorist Fr. Tomás de Santa María (c.1510-1570).[10]

Do not overuse graces. As Jean Baptiste Besard (translated by John Dowland) said: '*onely take heed, least in making too many shakes thou hinder the perfection of the Notes.*'[4]

A shake is a grace note that starts on the main note, moves to an auxiliary note a step above or below it, and then back again. This move can happen any number of times. The step above or below may be one fret or two, depending on the key and scale. Let us look at some different ways one could interpret a single chord shown with a shake.

The stave below shows a chord with the '#' that, to the experienced lutenist, opens up a world of possibilities. A few of many possible interpretations are shown in the measures that follow:

If course, deciding which kind of grace note to play and making a choice that fits the context is all part of musicianship. The most important thing to remember when playing graces is that they should be played with clarity and without losing the rhythm.

A fall starts on the auxiliary and moves to the main note. Again, this may be repeated as often as the lutenist wishes. The fall below could begin a step below the main note (also known as a *fore fall*, a *fall from below* or *apoggiatura from below*) or on the auxiliary one step above (also known as a *back fall*, a *fall from above* or an *apoggiatura from above*):

These are both what Mace[6] called *half falls*. What he called the *whole fall* (which he described as being out of fashion) only occurs from the 'd' upwards, when a second auxiliary may be used. He described it thus: *'in some Cases it is very Good, and Handsome, and may give Delight'*. The chord in the first measure below could be interpreted either as a half fall or a whole fall – it is shown here interpreted as a whole fall:

Martin Shepherd[9] speculates that the two crosses next to each other in an Almande by Robert Dowland, hand-written by his father John in Margaret Board's Lute Book, signify a whole fall. Interpretation seems to be all about context, but the most important thing of all is that the ornament is played beautifully. As Mace[6] said: *'For you must know This, That whatever your Grace be, you must, in your Fare-well, express the True Note perfectly, or else your pretended Grace, will prove a Disgrace.'*

VIBRATO

Vibrato was in and out of fashion at different points during the renaissance, and is noted in various texts. Capirola[8] appeared to describe notes with red dots above them as requiring vibrato, while later, the respected Parisian teacher and lutenist Jehan Basset referred to vibrato as *verre casse* and wrote that 'one of the reasons modern people have rejected it is because in the old days it was used almost all the time'[11] – something with which Mace[6] agreed. This implies that sparingly-used vibrato might be considered a good thing. In any case, I consider it a good thing and use it sparingly in my own performances.

Martin Shepherd[9] suggests that the cluster of dots (shown below, before the top treble note in the opening chord) seen in John Dowland's handwriting in Margaret Board's Lute Book signifies vibrato.

There are two forms of renaissance vibrato, the one-finger vibrato and the two or three fingered forms. The latter is simply a sort of very fast shake. The former is what we nowadays think of as vibrato. Mace described it: '*To perform it well, the finger of the left hand ought to be placed at the point indicated; and although the string will be played with the right hand, the left hand must swing with great violence, without lifting the fingertip from the string.*'[6]

Luys Venegas de Henestrosa, the Spanish vihuela composer, had an even better description of vibrato, using the word '*menear*' (that is, to shake or wiggle) to describe the motion of the finger on the fret.[12]

Normally, vibrato is not indicated in lute music, and like so many things appears to be left to the interpretation of the performer. This lack of complete certainty is one of the things I love about being a lutenist!

Right hand ornamentation really refers to two very different things: two types of changes to the music itself, and changes to the characteristics of the sound of the plucked string.

The first type of change to the written score is arpeggiation – the breaking up of a chord into its constituent notes, played quickly one after the other. Arpeggios are explained in more detail in the section on the 'Right Hand' where we examine 'Chord Plucking'.

DIVISIONS

Divisions, sets of variations, or (in Spain) *diferencias,* describe the diminution or repetition of a musical subject by breaking-down chords and longer notes into runs and notes of shorter duration. Sometimes, divisions also include temporary changes to compound meter. True divisions follow the original chord progression, mode and scale of the piece, but at times there may be deviation from this original form. Writing successful sets of divisions is an art form in itself.

The idea of divisions originates from the 15th century, but the first published divisions were in '*Los seys libros del delphin*' by the great Spanish composer Luys de Narváez[13], in 1538.

In England, divisions were particularly popular, and were seen throughout Elizabethan times both in the form of improvised variations on themes and also as pre-written sections on the repeats of strains. Most effective of all, perhaps, are some of the divisions that exist in duet treble parts. Divisions normally begin quite simply and become increasingly elaborate, providing shape, structure and texture to the music rather than allowing it to meander meaninglessly.

Here is the opening measure from the popular anonymous solo Packington's Pound Jig[14] with an example of a division around it.

Practice

Many people seem to confuse 'playing' with 'practice'. Simply put, practice is the hard work that makes you play music well.

It is important to establish your own personal practice routine, and stick to it so that progress in music becomes part of ordinary life. If your lifestyle changes dramatically, then of course you should adjust the practice routine. Practice routines vary dramatically from person to person, because everyone's concentration levels, abilities, speeds of progression, strengths, weaknesses and long-term aims are entirely personal to them. I would like you to make lute practice part of daily life rather than a possible postscript to the day that may be ignored if it is inconvenient. Once this is established, you will reap the rewards.

LONG-TERM AIMS

Your long-term aims determine how seriously you intend to pursue music and, in part, how much time you wish to allotted to it daily. This does not imply that someone who does not wish to perform concerts shouldn't spend most of their free time in practice; rather, it suggests that you should realistically divide your free time according to how important your various leisure activities are. If lute-playing is more than a hobby, then of course you need to find extra time for it. Optimum success is achieved when practice and ordinary life work in harmony with one another. Knowing your own aims is part of knowing yourself.

LENGTH OF PRACTICE

In my experience, most people practice at their best in bursts of around thirty minutes before a short break is advisable. This is good for both the body and mind. The amount of time you should spend practising in a day is entirely up to you as an individual. It depends on your levels of 'Lautenlust' (the desire you have to play) compared to the amount of time you have available. Of course, you should push yourself to practice even when your Lautenlust levels are low. The longer spent on quality practice, the better the student will probably become. Being realistic is perhaps the most important thing with practice: you will achieve far more in the long-term from two consistent, daily sessions of thirty minutes than from regularly intending to put in three hours of work but missing days at a time.

WORKING ALONE

Students working without a teacher who wish to improve need to:

▸ Decide on realistic goals, both short-term and long-term
▸ Recognise problems that may prevent the goal being achieved
▸ Work out how to overcome those problems
▸ Achieve the goal and then begin the process again

This applies to working on a piece of music, developing technique, or pretty much anything within the realm of improving as a musician.

DIVISION OF PRACTICE

Practice time should be divided up effectively, keeping everything as fresh as possible. If practice becomes boring, revise your approach. I tend to find it takes half an hour to examine a new three or four minute piece in detail, determine what work needs to be done, look at the technical issues surrounding it and write appropriate 'squiggles' on the music. After a break, I spend another half hour on in-depth work on recognised issues. By this point, a clear picture will emerge of how long it will take to learn to play a particular piece well. In the event of a 'rogue' session where nothing works, do something different and return to the problem refreshed.

SELF-CRITIQUE

Observe everything, and perfect that which is not exactly as it should be. This should be done in a positive way – any improvement is good. If you need to, make a check-list for things to look at. A non-exhaustive list might include seated position and posture, hand positions, fingerings, mechanics (see below), sound quality and interpretation.

MECHANICS

The mechanics of playing refers to the physical actions required to play the notes. In a move from one left hand position to another, for example, the order of the fingers may be vital to the fluency of the music; and the way in which they move will decide whether or not even the simplest note may be played beautifully. Equally, the plucking action – that is, the direction and amount of movement and depth of plucking – of the right hand affects not only the sound you make but also its ability to move accurately and quickly to the next position required.

ASK QUESTIONS

The more questions you ask of yourself and of others the more confidence and knowledge you will gain. Research, read, discuss and listen. Never be shy of asking someone with more experience than you for their opinions, but always remember that lute music has plenty of grey areas. If everybody had always done everything in exactly the same way, such greats as Francesco da Milano and John Dowland would never have stood out from the crowd as geniuses.

ONE-HANDED PRACTICE

When examining one part of technique on a piece of music, it can be very useful to play with one hand. It allows the brain to absorb the shapes and patterns in a more focused manner, and you can observe, criticise and improve one hand far more easily than two.

When observing the left hand, imagine the sounds whilst moving your fingers slowly and carefully. Watch the angle of your hand, the way the fingers move and the order they move in. Make sure that the fingering is correct, that you hold fingers on or move them off at appropriate times, and that your thumb is positioned correctly.

When observing the right hand, place a sock under the strings to deaden the sound, and imagine the notes in your head while plucking. Maintain a correct hand position and make sure your fingers move to the right courses at the right time. Check that your movements are fluid and that you do not have any unnecessary tension in your tendons.

SLOW PRACTICE

If I had to give a single piece of advice to students, it would be to practice slowly. Whether you are examining a single phrase or playing through an entire piece of music, full speed is a final aim, not a starting point. Practising too quickly is one of the biggest time-wasting exercises of all, and yet many students struggle with this, and end up with pieces that contain inaccuracies as a result.

If you practice phrases at a quarter speed to begin with, and then slowly increase the tempo, you will be able to examine your technique properly. This sort of discipline makes real musicians in the long-term.

Learning a Piece

Now let us get down to some more practical luting and examine how to go through a piece of music and learn to play it well.

This piece is from the well-known hand-written manuscript, Jane Pickering's Lute Book, which was begun in 1616. It is called 'A Toy', and was the first 'proper' piece of music I ever learned to play. While it is not technically particularly demanding, it still needs care and plenty of time taken with it in order to get it right.

Start as you mean to go on, and make sure you learn 'A Toy' accurately and carefully. I suggest you begin by producing a copy in your own handwriting, because it helps you notice every little detail about the piece. It can also be a very useful aid when trying to memorise music.

'A Toy' – Anon (Pickering)

Next, look at the piece in detail. Interpret and understand any marks on the music. Find out the meaning of anything you don't know.

Now, break down the rhythm: think of the fastest note as a '1' count. This makes the opening chord a '4', and the next note a '2'. Using a slash to separate measures, the opening section counts as follows:

4, 2 / 3, 1, 2 / 3, 1, 2 / 4, 2 / 3, 1, 2 / 3, 1, 2 / 4, 2 / 2, 2, 2
(the last measure has the same rhythm both 1st and 2nd time through).

Next we need good left and right hand fingerings. Fingering is vital. Always know what the left and right hands are supposed to do before trying to make them do it – or they won't be able to do it properly.

Let us now examine a good left hand fingering for the opening section of this piece. In the shorthand I have used, notes in a chord are shown with '&' in between with the highest notes indicated first, '0' indicates an open course, and slashes separate the measures. Individual notes are separated by commas.

1&0, 2 / 1, 3, 0 / 1&0, 0, 1 / 0&0, 0 / 1&0, 2, 0 / 0&0, 1, 3 / 4&0, 0 /
1st time: 1, 2, 0 /
2nd time: 1, 2, 3 /

Remember that there is often more than one good way to finger a piece, and deciding on a fingering is fundamental to good playing. Where possible, try to maintain the same style of fingering within a piece.

Have a go at working out a fingering for the second section now, and check it afterwards against a standard fingering as shown below.

1&0, 0 / 2, 0, 3 / 1&0, 0 / 2, 0, 3 / 1&0, 0 / 1, 3&0 / 4&0, 0 /
1st time: 1, 2, 3 /
2nd time: 1, 2, 0 /

The standard, as I mentioned earlier, is to write left hand fingering either next to the glyphs or underneath the stave. I suggest using a pencil to begin with, and then over-writing in pen once you are sure that everything works properly.

Next, you need a good right hand fingering, and to understand the pulse of the piece. Again, mark the accented notes in pencil to begin with.

If you refer to the section on 'The Right Hand', you will recall that accented two-note chords should be plucked using the right hand thumb (*p*) in conjunction with the middle finger (*m*); accented single notes should be plucked with the thumb (*p*) or middle finger (*m*), depending on the right hand technique used. Where two accented notes appear in succession, simply use the same digit again.

Here is a shorthand description of the accented notes for the opening section of 'A Toy'. An 'A' is a heavy accent, an 'a' is a light accent and a dash is no accent at all. On the music, mark the unaccented notes with a single dot to show the indice (*i*) plucking finger.

A- / A-a / A-a / A- / A-a / A-a / A- / 1st: A-a /; 2nd: A-a /.

The main accent is on the opening beat of each measure, and there is a secondary accent on the last note of each three-note measure.

Ignore any ornamentation until you have mastered the basic version of the piece. Now, try to play the piece through at a quarter speed. Refer to the various practice tips in this book, make a check-list, and go over anything that has doubt attached to it again and again, microscopically checking each tiny detail. Once you are able to play a slow version of the basic piece, look at the ornaments, and work on integrating them into the music.

It takes a fair amount of patience to get on top of everything in this slow, methodical way at first, but it soon becomes much easier to learn a piece in this way. A few pieces down the line, it becomes second nature.

When the music flows properly at about a quarter of the intended tempo, speed up very slightly and repeat until the required tempo has been achieved. You may be surprised at how quickly this is achieved.

It is important to find music of the right standard of difficulty and not to work on too many things simultaneously. Even now, I rarely work on more than a few pieces at a time. The beginner should focus on one piece at first, and learn it properly before moving on.

All About Exercises

In my opinion, there are few things as important in music-making as warming-up properly and using technique exercises to improve one's overall playing. As someone who had a tendon injury as a result of NOT warming-up when I was starting out, I thoroughly recommend doing it. All the professionals I know warm up before playing – and all amateurs SHOULD do. There are three main reasons:

▸ To help prevent injuries
▸ To increase blood flow and temperature to the hands
▸ To make the muscles in the hand feel ready to play

As such, most exercises may be used for warming-up. The important thing is that you exercise both the left and right hand fingers. Play through the exercise slowly, and pick up the speed slightly as you repeat it. The most important thing with warming-up is that you take your time, and carry on until the fingers and hands feel more elastic and move with ease.

For technique-building, exercises are an invaluable study aid. Concentrating on specific aspects of your playing without thinking about working on an entire piece allows the brain to focus; and it is easier to understand your own playing by recognising those exercises you find easier or harder. Those you find trickiest highlight potential weaknesses in your technique that you should consider improving.

I devote around fifteen minutes per session to technique building, and still watch my left and right hands carefully the first time through each one, to make sure that I am using the correct fingerings – something I advise you to do constantly until you can play the exercises well.

Do not try to play exercises fast. The idea is to play them correctly, which means slowly at first, carefully and with attention to detail.

So, here are a few short exercises for the left and right hands. More experienced players may decide to write their own or develop these to help improve weaknesses specific to them. Repeat them over and over until they become automatic and feel easy.

A SELECTION OF LEFT HAND EXERCISES

EXERCISE #1:
LH POSITION & CONTROL

Play the notes in pairs, leaving the initial finger on when adding the next. After playing each pair of notes remove the fingers as you begin the next sequence. Repeat the exercise in groups of four fingers. Pressing harder on the frets on notes 1 and 3 will make it seem easier.

EXERCISE #2:
BAR CHORDS & MECHANICS OF LH FINGER MOVEMENT

This exercise tests bar technique. I suggest that you re-read the section on bar chords before attempting it. It also requires good choices to be made about which fingers move where, and when. Try to keep your movements fluid and to think ahead if possible.

EXERCISE #3:
SLURS – HAMMERS AND PULL-OFFS

In order to achieve beautiful-sounding grace ornaments, slurring is a vital skill. Remember that accuracy is the key, and that in descending slurs (pull-offs) both fingers must be in place before the move begins. When you have mastered this exercise, try playing the same positions on courses 2 and 3.

EXERCISE #4:
LH POSITION, USE & POSITIONING OF LH FINGERS

In measures 1, 3, 5 and 7, add one finger per fret in turn without removing any until the end of the measure. In measures 2, 4, 6 and 8, only one finger moves – hold the others on until the end of the measure, then remove all fingers. Only try to understand those instructions when holding a lute!

A SELECTION OF RIGHT HAND EXERCISES

EXERCISE #5:
RH THUMB-FINGER ALTERATION TECHNIQUES

Use *p* for the first note and *i* for the second, then alternate throughout. The sound should be smooth and continuous, with a regular pulse. All players should build a solid thumb-finger alternation technique.

EXERCISE #6:
PRACTISING TRIPLETS

Thumb-finger aficionados may use *p-i-p*, or *p-i-p* followed by *i-p-i*; medio-indice players might use *m-i-m*, or *m-i-m* followed by *i-m-i*. Whichever you prefer, three of the triplet notes make up a single beat: make sure you maintain the accent on the first note in each set of three. Start slowly and speed up each time you play through the exercise.

EXERCISE #7:
RH TECHNIQUES, USING VARIED PLUCKING PATTERNS

I believe it is important to have complete control of the right hand, and this exercise tests your right hand control. The fingering has been included, except for the final chord. Try using all the different chord-plucking techniques for 6 note chords in turn.

EXERCISE #8:
CHORD-PLUCKING TECHNIQUES

Before attempting this chordal exercise, re-read the section on chord plucking, decide on your right hand fingering, and then follow it carefully. There are decisions to be made about when using *i, m* and *a* might be better than *i, m* and *p*.

Repertoire

There could be up to 30,000 pieces of lute music in existence, and no one knows how many more have been lost. There is certainly enough repertoire to keep a lutenist going for several lifetimes! Initially, I suggest that beginners should invest in a few books of easy, short pieces of music.

The Lute Society of Great Britain (www.lutesociety.org) currently publishes a number of useful student aids that are available online from their website, and Peacock Press have a wonderful stock of lute books too. I recommend these editions for beginners, available which are online from the Lute Society:

- ▸ 58 Very Easy Pieces
- ▸ 40 Easy to Early Intermediate Pieces
- ▸ 70 Easy to Intermediate Pieces
- ▸ 114 Early to Intermediate Pieces

Just a small note on pre-printed fingerings: It is always worth exercising a little caution before simply accepting them. Apart from anything else, there is often more than one way to finger a piece well, mistakes are easily made, and people often have different fingering styles to one another. I don't like all the fingerings in the above books, but they are great value for money, providing over 250 short, simple pieces in total.

You might wish to look at some of my own editions (published by Peacock Press and available online at www.amazon.co.uk as well as via my website at www.bensalfield.com) which include 'A Collection of Renaissance Solos' – 20 basic pieces playable by relative beginners, with sets of new divisions that will challenge those who have been playing for several years.

These sorts of publications will give a taster of some of the variety of available lute repertoire. After a few weeks of looking through this material, you may start to have a clearer picture of the styles, eras, composers or even countries whose music you wish to study more closely. This in turn may influence your long-term technique and help formulate an overall overall direction.

Performance

For many people who play the lute, talking about performance is an irrelevance. For a few people, who are both willing and able to present lute music to an audience, it seems relevant to talk about some ideas and principles surrounding performance.

GENERAL TIPS

It is important to find out who you are as a performer, and to enjoy presenting the music in your own way. I spent the first couple of decades of my professional performing career with half an eye on what other people would think of me. Will the reviewer enjoy my Dowland? What will the famous classical guitarist in row two think about my interpretation of the Bach suite? Nowadays I do not worry. After all, people will either like it, or not. Those who go to hear a lute concert usually go for one of very few reasons:

- They like the performer
- They like lute music
- Curiosity
- They fancy a night out
- They are supportive of their local arts scene
- There's nothing on TV

Whichever of these reasons motivates audience members to attend, the chances are that if the performer gives their all and is reasonably likeable, the listeners will enjoy themselves – and that's what they are there to do.

A few things worth considering:

- Make sure your concert length is roughly what people expect
- Always leave your audience wanting a bit more of you
- It is often best to play shorter pieces together in a group
- Look for ways to tie parts of the programme together
- Contrast and compare music where possible
- If you speak, address the back of the hall, slowly and clearly
- Building a rapport with an audience gets rid of nerves
- Take your time with everything – there is no need to rush

PUTTING TOGETHER A PROGRAMME

There is no right or wrong way to put a programme together – but there are certainly good and bad programmes! Sometimes I may be asked to perform specific music – for example, Elizabethan dance tunes by Dowland or Sonatas by Weiss – but usually I have a completely free rein over the content.

A good programme has a certain amount of structure, with an introduction, a middle and an conclusion. If there is an interval, each half should be treated in this way. Varying mood, tempo, composers and styles is all worth the deepest consideration. Twenty fast galliards in the same key and style may start to lose their charm before half way, even if the music itself is of the highest quality.

From a performance point of view, it is good to begin with music you know well. It gives you time to settle in and relax about what you are doing. In a varied programme with an interval in the middle, I often aim for three groups per half, with the longest parts in the middle, and the most dramatic at the end. I consider it rather passé to finish on the fastest and most complicated piece in one's repertoire, and instead I often end with something that has emotive power. In 2014, for instance, I finished about twenty concerts with my transcription of the amazing 'Tombeau sur la morte de M. Comte d'Losy' by Weiss – in its full glory, with dark, anguished shadows and raw pain attached!

If I play a concert where there is only one composer, I look for contrasts in the music, especially if there are suites or sonatas involved. Alternatively, if the pieces are short, I might try the exact opposite and try to link music together in a hypnotic fashion.

It's worth remembering that audiences often respond well to succinct, friendly introductions. I tend to talk for a couple of minutes about each group of pieces, and try to include an interesting or amusing anecdote during the spiel. If you can raise a laugh, you will certainly raise a clap.

A professional player is only ever a handful of dreadful concerts away from the end of his or her career – but no one plays brilliantly every concert. The main thing is to make sure the audience is entertained… and they probably will be if you yourself enjoy what you are doing.

PRE-CONCERT ROUTINE

Most performers tend to develop a pre-concert routine. This can include how much and when they practice on the day of a recital, when and what they eat and drink, when they change into their concert clothes and how long before performing they like to arrive at the venue.

Such routines are important because they give the performer a feeling of security, which in turn makes them feel more relaxed and, ultimately, perform better.

A few tips for the novice performer:

▸ Never over-practice on a concert day. If you go past your peak, you will perform with tired muscles and tendons. I tend to practice for no more than an hour on a concert day.
▸ Look at the important bits of the music. Play through the start of the concert, top-and-tail the rest of the pieces, have a look at any especially tricky parts, and then relax a bit.
▸ Be careful not to eat too much before performing. Food and nerves combine badly – your audience is not paying to see a nauseous, tired person playing lute music for them!

THE CONCERT

By the time you actually sit down to perform, you may feel quite nervous – a completely natural and normal reaction. The most important thing to do is to focus. There is no point in worrying while you should be performing – just give everything your best shot. If your programme is well prepared, you should know your 'opening gambit' inside out, and the first applause should help settle the nerves.

If the audience is very small, self-doubt can creep in. Don't let it. Tiny audiences do not reflect on your ability as a performer but on the promoter's ability to promote properly. Just make sure you do your job well and allow him or her to regret their own failings!

If the audience is huge, the enormity of the situation may hit you. Just focus on someone towards the back, present your concert to them, and enjoy the sound of a large crowd of people applauding you at the end!

THE NICETIES OF PERFORMANCE

The way a concert performer dresses for a concert and interacts with an audience is normally dependant on a number of factors such as the formality or otherwise of the occasion, the size of the audience and the artist's own individual style. When everything fits together nicely, there is a comfortable feeling; but a lack of awareness of how things ought to be done may leave an audience feeling uncomfortable and the performer looking a little bit silly.

Bowing is a sign of respect for an audience before the concert begins, and the musician's way of saying 'thank you for the clapping' after applause. It is easy to bow: just keep your hands by your sides and bend slightly from the waist. Normally, the longer the applause, the deeper and longer the bow – and the applause tends to be longer after a twenty minute sonata than after a two-minute piece stand-alone piece.

Usually, an audience in the UK will politely applaud even if they are not taken with the concert. There are exceptions, of course. Conductor Michael Tilson Thomas once recalled the première of Steve Reich's work, 'Four Organs', at Carnegie Hall in 1973, where a woman apparently walked down the aisle and banged her head against the front of the stage, crying 'Stop, stop! I confess!'

After enjoying part of the applause at the end of a concert, a performer traditionally leaves the stage or performance area. If the applause continues, he or she returns and bows and nods before sitting down again to play an encore. I always leave a second time before the encore – some call it 'milking', but I see it as a game between audience and performer where the social rules are in place, the outcome is already known, and the enjoyment of the moment is being shared by both parties. It can go wrong of course: once I saw a pianist wait a few seconds too long and have to rush back on stage to 'steal' an encore when the applause started to die down. He tripped on the step to the polished, wooden stage and slid across it, face down.

Except in very exceptional circumstances – when your name is being chanted to slow-clapping, for example – you should not give a second encore. They really must be demanded by an audience, and desperation is never attractive in a concert performer.

AFTER THE CONCERT

It is often the case that, following a concert, some aficionados will come and have a few words with the performer. I recommend that concert artists, however mentally and physically destroyed they feel, should spend a few minutes talking to anyone who wishes to interact with them. Pleasantries cost nothing, and it is always heartening when someone praises your interpretation of a suite or a piece that you thought you had made a complete mess of! Try not to make anyone wait too long and always smile nicely, shake hands in a friendly manner and make each person feel welcome and important – because, simply, they are! Lute audience are not the biggest or easiest to find, so we should be grateful that people wish to spend their time listening to us, however wonderful our playing might be.

SOME PEOPLE CANNOT PERFORM

My final word one performance is simply to point out that performance is not the be-all and end-all, the pinnacle of achievement, or even relevant to most people, and it should not be the perceived ultimate end result for everyone who can play at a high level.

Some people can play brilliantly but are unable to perform; conversely, a few of us – for whom the fates have conspired to lead us into the path of professional performance – may actually play better in front of an audience. I know for a fact that I put my music across best when there are people listening.

There are a million reasons for an inability to perform for an audience – from acute nervousness or a shy personality to physical things such as shaking, sweaty hands. I know a lutenist who performs, but who cannot talk to his audience without his voice becoming incredibly shrill; I know a guitarist who looks incredibly confident and plays to a very high level, but who will only play in duo – because the pressure of solo performance makes him fall apart.

The thing to remember is what is important, and that is the music. As long as you enjoy playing it, if it fulfils something inside you to be able to have it in your life, then it is worthwhile – whether you play for yourself in your bedroom, for your family and friends, or for massive concerts at international festivals, at the end of the day we are all just lutenists on this mortal coil for a limited amount of time!

My Early Lute Years

I first played a lute on my thirteenth birthday. My teacher, Ian Thomson, left Cornwall the following summer and after that I was pretty much on my own. I quickly developed a highly efficient and effective set of autodidactic principles and a fearsome streak of determination.

My approach to life has always been pragmatic, and I quickly realised that in order to succeed I had both to develop my playing to a high standard and to lay the foundations for a career in the music industry. With no practical advice available, it was simply a matter of trial-and-error, learning from errors and grafting to get to where I wanted to be.

My method of learning was something that I am still proud of, because the fundamental principles were correct and still apply both to my teaching and learning. I developed an ability to self-criticise harshly and accurately, and to notice and correct errors quickly. I studied medical books to learn about the make-up of the hand, and worked out the most efficient ways to use them on a lute. My three-hours minimum daily practice was very structured, and by the time I was seventeen, I was a good player, and possibly the youngest concert lutenist in Europe.

I had already been told by various people who could have been helpful to me that it was impossible to make a living out of lute music, so I decided to ignore all that, got out my typewriter and wrote to ten thousand people in the music industry nationally telling them everything I could about myself, from 1986-9. The idea was simple: if enough people at least knew my name, my path would be easier later on. It worked: by the early 1990s quite a few people in the music world nationally knew my name even if they couldn't place who I was, and the letters directly reaped a total of six concerts and a TV appearance!

As I approached 17, I wrote to the Bishop of Truro and asked him if he could advise me of a church where I could perform – church concerts being so popular here in Cornwall. He put me in touch with Father Leah at St Ives Parish Church of St Ia, and suddenly, in December 1988, came the debut. I will never forget the fear, the hand-written notes, the expectant audience (astonishingly, sixty-five people showed up) and my first experiences of everything. I hungered for more.

St Ia's is where I first met my dear friend the lutenist and scholar Denys Stephens, who is still a duo partner and sometime adviser of mine – and someone to whom I owe a debt of gratitude.

Next, I asked to give a short recital at the Lute Society meeting in February 1989. The day started badly: I left my lute on the dining table at home but still made it to Queen's Square with half an hour to spare. This was also the first of a small number of times in my life when I experienced being so depersonalised whilst performing that I felt I was a spectator. Each time, my playing standard has fortunately far exceeded my actual ability! I received a big ovation, so it turned out alright.

My third recital, that summer, was in my home town of Truro, at the Cathedral Chapter House. The audience was miserably small, but the West Briton newspaper gave me my first review: 'Performance of Real Perfection' shouted the headline, and it was full of comments such as 'bears comparison to such master lutenists as Julian Bream'. I realised then that even kindly reviewers don't often have a clue!

At that concert I made friends with half the audience. My late friend Kate Evans and the historian and author Steph Haxton were just two of the people there who would later affect my life positively.

Kate was a local music scene person who knew a few people, including the conductor Sir Roger Norrington, for whom I played a couple of times. I was heartened by his encouragement, and through him met and played for the late Sir Charles Groves. We both had 'flu and had been drinking brandy, which made us excellent company! He told his friend Julian Bream about me, and JB invited me for tea and said very complimentary things about my playing. I still have a number of letters from him. Oddly, the one thing he arranged for me, a BBC Radio 3 audition interview, didn't come to anything. On my way there I ran over a field mouse in my car and was so upset that I drove straight home and went to bed.

Then the local Beeb interviewed me at home. The lovely Juliet Morris, I remember. David Blount, Director of the Dawlish Arts Festival, saw me on TV and booked me for the 1992 Festival – my first festival booking, and a friend of Kate's announced that she had a relative who ran a music series at an abbey in Germany. Suddenly I was playing for hundreds and had become an 'international' concert performer.

While Dawlish was my first festival booking, it was not actually my first festival appearance. In 1989, over breakfast, my brother Jon and I had set up our own music festival. It was all arranged in a few hours – Michael Palmer, vicar of Devoran, provided the venue and we invited all our musical friends to play. Music promotion is still something I do.

My first proper, major international tour was booked for 1996 in the Czech Republic. Unfortunately, it coincided with their first parliamentary elections, and several of my shows were cancelled last minute. My total net earnings for the tour turned out to be negative, so I needed a plan of action and I needed one fast. After the last night, I went up to Prague where I remembered seeing an 8-ball pool hall. I knew that as long as I was at Želivského bus station the next afternoon I could meet the London coach, and planned to make some money on the baize.

There were a few very rich but not very good pool players there, and in those days I ran an 8-ball pool league. While I was not the best player, I certainly had enough tricks to handle this crowd. Game on...

At 4am I realised with a bit of a shiver that I had won the equivalent of over £900, and I could smell a certain amount of discontent in the air. Realising that I was in a potentially rather dangerous situation, I went to the toilets, climbed through the window – with my lute and travel bag... and just ran like the wind. I hid out for a while and then waited at Želivského, but I didn't mind too much – I was alive and had nearly a thousand quid in cash in my pocket!

I have to say, I do not regret a single moment of my life, although I confess I could and probably should have done many things differently; but we are no more than the sum of our own experiences with a splash of realisation. Nowadays, I live a relatively sedate life tucked away in the heart of the Cornish countryside. I only leave here to go and tour – so there's no more living on the edge, escaping dangerous situations, getting involved in duels or anything else anymore!

This was part of my personal route to notoriety; yours will doubtless be filled with practice, good decisions and good luck. I sincerely hope that this book helps you in your own musical quest, whatever that may be, and wish you good luck and happy luting!

References

1   *Ephemerides* - Samuel Hartlib (1659).

2   *The Schoole of Musicke* - Thomas Robinson (1603).

3   *Libro Secondo* - Franciscus Bossinensis (1511).

4   *A Varietie of Lute Lessons* - Robert Dowland (1610).

5   *David van Ooijen's website: www.davidvanooijen.nl*

6   *Musicke's Monument* - Thomas Mace (1676).

7   *English Lute Duets of the Golden Age: The Ultimate Collection* - Ben Salfield (2015).

8   *Capirola Lute Book* - Vincenzo Capirola [compiled by Vitale] (1520).

9   *The interpretation of signs for graces in English lute music* - Martin Shepherd, The Lute, vol. XXXVI (1996).

10 *Libro llamado arte de tañer fantasia* - Tomás de Santa María (1565).

11 *Harmonie Universelle* - Marin Marsenne [written by Jehan Basset] (1636).

12 *Libro de Cifra Nueva para tecla, harpa y vihuela* - Luis Venegas de Henestrosa (1557).

13 *Los seys libros delphín* - Luys de Narváez (1538).

14 *A Collection of Renaissance Solos* - Ben Salfield (2015).

15 *Intavolatura di Liuto e di Chitarrone* - Alessandro Piccinini (1632).

16 *Henry V, Act 3 Scene 6* - William Shakespeare (c.1599).

17 *Stobäus Manuscript* - Johann Stobäus (c.1619).

18 *On the right hand fingerings in lute publications of Nicolas Vallet* - Dmitri Goldobin, Nauchnyj vestnik Moskovskoj konservatorii (2009).

19 *Libro de música para vihuela intitulado Orphenica Lyra* - Miguel de Fuenllana (1554)

20 *Divisions, vol 1, no. iii* - Bruce MacEvoy (1979), (Lute Society of America, 2008).

21 *The Beginner's Guide to the Classical Guitar* – Jeffrey Goodman (2009)

22 *Intabolatura de lauto libro quarto* - Ottaviano Petrucci, (1508).

Ben Salfield's Editions

(All published by Peacock Press unless otherwise stated)

5-4-10: Five Preludes for Andrea Dieci by Ben Salfield
Modran Editions, Poland
[for classical guitar, in notation]

Fugue BWV 1000 by J.S. Bach (PLS 001)
[for 10-course lute, in tablature]

S.L. Weiss: Performance Versions of Selected Lute Works (PLS 002)
[for 10-course lute, in tablature]

A Collection of Renaissance Solos arr. by Ben Salfield (PLS 003)
[for 6-course+ lute or guitar, in tablature]

John Dowland: Complete Solo Galliards (PLS 004)
[for 6-course+ lute or guitar, in tablature]

Prelude, Fugue & Allegro BWV 998 by J.S. Bach (PLS 005)
[for 10-course lute, in tablature]

Suite BWV 997 by J.S. Bach (PLS 006)
[for 10-course lute, in tablature]

Concerto in D Major RV 93 by Antonio Vivaldi (PLS 007)
[for 6-course+ lute or guitar, two violins & bass continuo, in notation for all
instruments plus tablature for lute (4 tunings) and guitar]

English Lute Duets of the Golden Age: The Ultimate Collection arr. by
Ben Salfield (PLS 008) [for two 6-course+ lutes or guitars, in tablature]

AVAILABLE NOW FROM
Peacock Press via
www.amazon.co.uk and www.bensalfield.com

Lightning Source UK Ltd.
Milton Keynes UK
UKHW021508201119
353887UK00003B/16/P